Diary of a Ballerina

Angela Royston

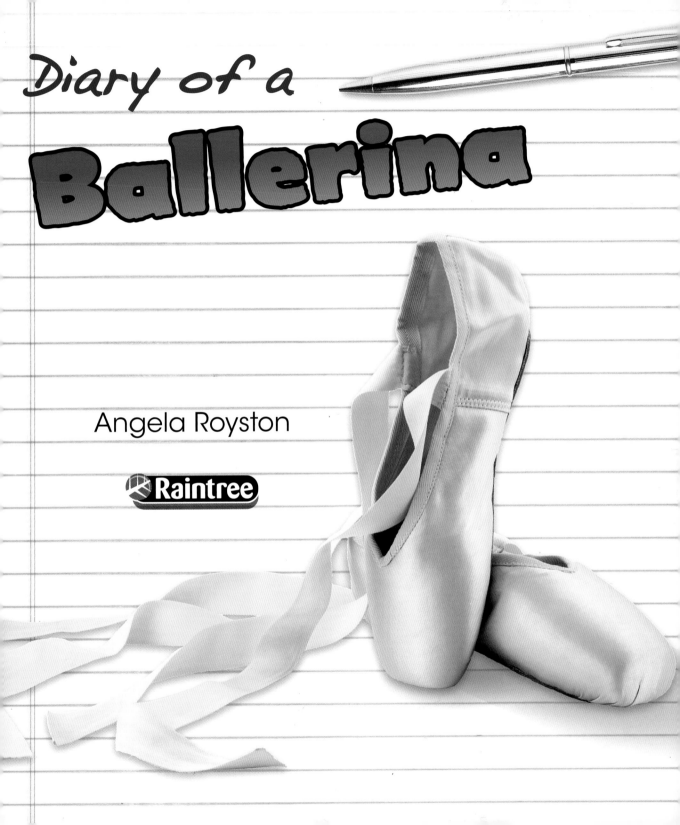

Raintree

Raintree is an imprint of Capstone Global Library Limited, a company incorporated in England and Wales having its registered office at 7 Pilgrim Street, London, EC4V 6LB – Registered company number: 6695582

To contact Raintree:
Phone: 0845 6044371
Fax: + 44 (0) 1865 312263
Email: myorders@raintreepublishers.co.uk
Outside the UK please telephone +44 1865 312262

Text © Capstone Global Library Limited 2014
First published in hardback in 2014
The moral rights of the proprietor have been asserted.

Edited by Daniel Nunn, Rebecca Rissman, and Catherine Veitch
Designed by Cynthia Della-Rovere
Picture research by Ruth Blair
Production by Victoria Fitzgerald
Originated by Capstone Global Library Ltd
Printed and bound in China by South China Printing Company Ltd

ISBN 978 1 406 26063 2
17 16 15 14 13
10 9 8 7 6 5 4 3 2 1

British Library Cataloguing in Publication Data
Royston, Angela.
Diary of a ballerina.
792.8-dc23
A full catalogue record for this book is available from the British Library.

Acknowledgements
We would like to thank the following for permission to reproduce photographs: Corbis pp. 8 (© Yuan Xue Jun/Redlink), 17 (© Robbie Jack), 20 (© Nathalie Darbellay/Sygma), 22 (© Yang Liu), 23 (© Bettmann); Getty Images pp. 5 (Washington Post), 7 (Hybrid Images), 9 (Maria Teijeiro), 11 (BENHAMOU/DUFOUR/Gamma-Rapho), 14 (David Fischer), 16 (DIETER NAGL/AFP), 18 (Sven Creutzmann/Mambo Photo/), 26 (Wendy Maeda/The Boston Globe), 27 (KIMMO MANTYLA/AFP); Shutterstock pp. title page (© Yuganov Konstantin), contents page, 21 (© Yuri Arcurs), 4, 25 (© Igor Bulgarin), 6 (© Felix Mizioznikov), 10 (© Cyhel), 13 (© Olesia Bilkei), 19 (© testing), 28 (© eans), 30 (© Brent Hofacker); Superstock pp. 12 (Ingram Publishing), 15 (Image Source), 24 (Stock Connection).

Background and design features reproduced with permission of Shutterstock. Cover photograph of ballerina stretching at barre reproduced with permission of Corbis (© Image Source).

We would like to thank Annie Besarra for her invaluable help in the preparation of this book.

Every effort has been made to contact copyright holders of material reproduced in this book. Any omissions will be rectified in subsequent printings if notice is given to the publisher.

All the Internet addresses (URLs) given in this book were valid at the time of going to press. However, due to the dynamic nature of the Internet, some addresses may have changed, or sites may have changed or ceased to exist since publication. While the author and publisher regret any inconvenience this may cause readers, no responsibility for any such changes can be accepted by either the author or the publisher.

Some words are shown in bold, **like this**. You can find out what they mean by looking in the Glossary.

Contents

My diary

Friday 12 June – seven days to go!

I'm so excited, because there are just seven days before our new ballet opens. The ballet is called *The Nutcracker*, and I am dancing the **role** of the Sugar Plum Fairy.

We have been **rehearsing** in the studio for weeks. The final week is always very busy.

Practice at the barre

Saturday 13 June – six days to go!

I practised this morning, as I do every single day. I **warmed up** at the **barre**. If I don't warm up carefully, I could injure myself. That would be a disaster!

Warming-up exercises help to warm up my muscles.

When I am **en pointe**, I balance on the tips of my toes in special shoes.

Then I practised my pointe work. I practised for longer than usual today, because I want to be at my very best for the performance.

Centre work

When I finished my **barre** exercises, I moved into the centre of the floor. Here I practised balancing, turning, jumping, and moving my whole body.

I finished with **cooling-down** exercises. These are as important as **warming up**. I love dancing, even when I am only practising.

The theatre

Sunday 14 June – five days to go!

Today we went to look around the theatre where we will be performing. I looked at the empty seats and imagined what it would be like when they were full of people.

A dancer gets ready in the dressing room.

I did a few **pirouettes** on the stage before we went backstage. The dressing rooms have just been redecorated. They look amazing!

Talking to students

Monday 15 June – four days to go!

Today I talked to a class of ballet students about how ballet dancers look on stage. We wear special stage make-up. Our hair must be neat and pulled back off our faces.

Ballerinas often put on their own make-up.

Ballet dancers have to look after themselves
when they are not dancing. As well as
exercising, I always make sure I eat plenty
of healthy food.

Hard work

Tuesday 16 June – three days to go!

A young girl asked me for my autograph as I left the studio. She asked me how I became a dancer. I told her I started ballet lessons when I was six years old.

I applied to join a ballet school when I was 12. I was nervous at the **audition**, and very happy when I was accepted.

Joining a ballet company

When I left ballet school, I joined a big ballet company as a member of the *corps de ballet*. It was so exciting!

Carlos Acosta

Then I joined a smaller ballet company, where I now dance **solo** parts.

My ambition is to get bigger **roles**. I would love to dance with Carlos Acosta – he is my favourite male dancer!

Dress rehearsal

Wednesday 17 June - two days to go!

We moved into the theatre today. We practised on the stage this morning. This evening we had a full **dress rehearsal** with the orchestra.

We wore our costumes and danced
the whole ballet as though it was a real
performance. There was even an audience,
including some of my friends and family.

Final fitting

Thursday 18 June – one day to go!

My costume felt a bit uncomfortable last night, so today I went to see the costume fitters. They were very busy today. There were **tutus** everywhere!

Then I tried on two new pairs of shoes that I bought for the opening performance tomorrow. They fitted well, which was a relief.

Last minute changes

The **choreographer** made some changes, too. He is the person who directs every step and move in the dance. He thought some of the movements needed more space on the stage.

George Balanchine

This meant we all had to change our positions. Sometimes I think he sees himself as George Balanchine – the most famous choreographer ever!

The curtain rises

Friday 19 June – First Night!

Today I was very excited and nervous, but doing my usual practice exercises helped to calm me down. Waiting for the performance to begin seemed to last forever.

At last the music started, the curtain went up, and the ballet began. I watched from the **wings** and waited. When the music for my dance began, I entered the stage.

Cheering and clapping

The music took me over and I danced as beautifully as I could. I wanted the audience to feel what the Sugar Plum Fairy felt.

At the end of the ballet, we all lined up on stage to make our final bows. People kept on clapping and cheering. The main dancers were given bouquets of flowers. It was so thrilling!

Writing a diary

You can write a diary, too! Your diary can describe your life – what you saw, what you felt, and the events that happened. You could even write an imaginary diary for one of your pets!

Writing a diary is a great way to help us remember the things that happened in our lives. You could pretend that your diary is a secret diary and begin with "Dear Diary"!

Here are some tips for writing a diary:

- Start each entry with the day and the date. You don't have to include an entry for every day.

- The entries should be in **chronological** order, which means that they follow the order in which events happened.

- Use the past tense when you are writing about something that has already happened.

- Remember that a diary is the writer's story, so use "I" and "my".

Glossary

audition test which includes performing. Dancers, actors, and other performers audition for parts, or to be accepted into special schools.

barre long rail, often in front of a mirror, that ballet dancers hold onto while they practise

choreographer person who decides all the steps in a dance

chronological in order of time

cooling-down (exercises) exercises that allow your body to gently relax

corps de ballet group of dancers who dance together

dress rehearsal practice performance of a whole ballet, from start to finish. In a dress rehearsal, the dancers wear their costumes.

en pointe when a ballerina balances and dances on the tips of her toes, wearing special shoes

pirouette twirl or spin

rehearse practise performing something

role part (or character) in a ballet, play, film, or other performance

solo performance by a dancer on his or her own

tutu short, stiff skirt worn by a ballerina

warm up (exercises) exercises that gently move the parts of your body you are about to use

wings places at the sides of the stage which the audience cannot see

Find out more

Books

Ballet Dance (Snap Books), Karen M. Graves (Capstone Press, 2008)

Ballet Dancer (Stage School), Lisa Regan (Windmill Books, 2012)

Love to Dance Ballet, Angela Royston (Raintree, 2012)

Mad About Ballet (Ladybird Minis), Lisa Regan (Ladybird, 2008)

Websites

www.ballet.org.uk
The website of the English National Ballet.

www.roh.org.uk
The website of the Royal Opera House in London, which includes the stories of famous ballets.

www.scottishballet.co.uk
This website includes photos, interviews, and videos of performances.

Index